The Ultimate Guide To Start Your Own Cake Business

How To Start And Develop A Cake Business

Catherine Joyce

Table of Contents

Introduction

Chapter 1: Laying the Ground

Chapter 2: Develop Your Flavor Palette

Chapter 3: Business Requirements

Chapter 4: Marketing and Promotion

Chapter 5: Logistics

Chapter 6: Continue to Grow

Chapter 7: Explore the industry

Conclusion

Introduction

I want to thank you and congratulate you for downloading the book, *The Ultimate Guide to Start Your Own Cake Business: How to Start and Develop a Cake Business"*.

This book contains proven steps and strategies on how to start and run your own cake business.

It will guide you through every aspect of establishing your cake shop—from perfecting the flavors you will offer, up to the technical and legal matters involved in running a business. Marketing and promotion for the expansion of your client base and the business itself will be discussed as well.

But it does not end with being able to put up and run the business. The book also talks about challenging yourself to expand your horizon. It encourages you to achieve continuous growth while citing examples on how to do so. It gives valuable insight as to the importance of tirelessly working to perfect your craft.

Thanks again for purchasing this book, I hope you enjoy it!

© **Copyright 2014 by Catherine Joyce - All rights reserved.**

This document is geared towards providing exact and reliable information in regards to the topic and issue covered. The publication is sold with the idea that the publisher is not required to render accounting, officially permitted, or otherwise, qualified services. If advice is necessary, legal or professional, a practiced individual in the profession should be ordered.

- From a Declaration of Principles which was accepted and approved equally by a Committee of the American Bar Association and a Committee of Publishers and Associations.

In no way is it legal to reproduce, duplicate, or transmit any part of this document in either electronic means or in printed format. Recording of this publication is strictly prohibited and any storage of this document is not allowed unless with written permission from the publisher. All rights reserved.

The information provided herein is stated to be truthful and consistent, in that any liability, in terms of inattention or otherwise, by any usage or abuse of any policies, processes, or directions contained within is the solitary and utter responsibility of the recipient reader. Under no circumstances will any legal responsibility or blame be held against the publisher for any reparation, damages, or monetary loss due to the information herein, either directly or indirectly.

Respective authors own all copyrights not held by the publisher.

The information herein is offered for informational purposes solely, and is universal as so. The presentation of the information is without contract or any type of guarantee assurance.

The trademarks that are used are without any consent, and the publication of the trademark is without permission or backing by the trademark owner. All trademarks and brands within this book are for clarifying purposes only and are the owned by the owners themselves, not affiliated with this document.

Chapter 1: Laying the Ground

To get started on anything—business, recreation, hobby, or job-it is important that you do your research first. This way, you will know how to work your way around properly without missing essential points. Also, starting a business is quite tricky, especially since it involves a long term investment. So you really have to do your homework and find out all the factors that play into running your own cake shop. This includes all aspects—from the taste and presentation of the cakes, to the logistics, equipment and facilities, legal papers and permits, marketing and promotion, expenses, etc. Remember, you have to master and prepare all these before your big launch.

Another factor to consider here is that there is a difference if you want to run an online business from your home, or if you plan to open your own cake shop or store front. They certainly have varying legal requirements. There are differences as well in expenses and logistics. Even the demands from the baker, day-to-day operations, and workload can vary greatly.

Apart from these, you should dig deeper as well into what constitutes running your own cake business in your area. There are states which have more stringent measures and pose additional requirements. You have to take note of those, especially when you expand.

Essentially, there are three main aspects to focus on: taste, business, and logistics. Each of these will be discussed in the succeeding chapters.

Chapter 2: Develop Your Flavor Palette

First on the list is the flavor palette of your cake shop. This is the core of your business. You are in the food industry. Hence, your primary priority should be perfecting the taste and flavors of your cakes. There are thousands of competitors in this industry. Hence, you have to find out what will give you the edge that will leave people craving for your products.

Flavor palette

One of the first things that you have to prepare before you open your cake business is your flavor palette. This involves the designs and recipes you offer, the cakes themselves. With the stiff competition in the industry, you have to find something that will make you unique, something that will make you stand out. The fact is, cake businesses are everywhere. Certain flavors have already become a staple, and a lot of business executives and pastry chefs have cut out a niche for themselves.

Given this, what more will you still be able to offer that will attract cake lovers to your shop's doors (or website in online cake shops)? Will you bank on the "oomph" in the taste of your cakes? Will you be developing your very own mix of flavors? Will you tackle the competition with extravagant presentation? Or will you be doing simple cakes that have a homemade appeal which will make prospective customers think of home?

Remember, this is all about taste and presentation. It starts with the mastery of these two factors. After all, they are the core of your business.

Recipes

One of the first things on your plate is developing your recipes. Part of opening your own cake business is developing your own recipe.

This does not mean though that everything in your menu must be new flavors. When it comes to cakes, there are certain flavors that people will always look for. Hence, you always have to offer them. These are the basic flavors—chocolate, vanilla, red velvet, carrot cake, something fruity, and a special flavor (like Nutella, Toblerone or Cookie Butter cake).

Even though these are already basic flavors which have been offered by cake shops for the longest time, it does not mean that you cannot tweak them. You can come up with your own modified recipe so that you still make it your own—then that will be your selling point as well. You will have your very own version of the Red Velvet or Decadent Chocolate Cake. You can experiment with fillings, custards, or some other parts of the recipe.

Aside from these basic flavors, you will have to have your very own flavors and mixes. For instance, you can have strawberry banana chocolate cake. Or you can have honey carrot cheesecake. It is up to you. Make the flavors pop. Remember, variety is a vital factor to consider here. You may have the best flavors, but if they are limited, your customers will soon get tired of them.

With that, it is also a good idea to develop new recipes on a regular basis—like monthly for example. This will also give your clients something new to look forward to. But of course, do not ever let go of your staples. Distinguish your staple flavors, which by the way, you also have to choose.

Last but not least, do not forget to come up with your signature cake. This will be your trademark, your main distinguishing factor that will make you stand out from other cake businesses. Do not rush this though because it will surely take time. You ought to remember that this is your signature cake. Hence, it must be the best out of all the cakes you offer. This must be your best seller, a must try in your menu, one of the reasons why your customers will keep coming back to you.

Keep in mind that recipes are a matter of trial and error. It takes time to perfect them, so do not ever rush them.

Presentation

Pay particular attention to presentation. Again, you eat with your eyes first. If yours is not an heirloom business that has been handed down from one generation to the next, or you have not established a name yet, presentation becomes much more important because this is the first thing that your potential clients will see. Thus, your presentation must not only be distinct, it must be enticing enough to make even non-cake lovers drool.

Another thing that you ought to bear in mind is that the presentation must match the overall theme of your cake business. Say for instance your theme is homemade. Accordingly, the presentation of your cakes must be simple yet beautiful. They must be able to remind your customers of the cake that their moms used to make. On the other hand if you opt to have a gourmet cake business, then you should experiment with more classy or extravagant designs. The same parallelism should be in place whether you offer wedding cakes, baby cakes, or kinky cakes.

Given all this, it is a must to master your cake decorating skills. You must also be versatile enough to pull off the design demands from your clients. There are different frosting strokes and techniques. You can play with various decorating tools as well. So do not be afraid to experiment. You can also watch videos online to serve as your peg.

Catchy name

The name of your cakes will also be a factor to consider here. Having unique and catchy names is a good way to promote your goods and have name recall. Just make sure though that the name speaks of the character and taste of the cake. For instance, a particular cake business named their nutty cake Nuts About You. So right off the bat, you know that the cake is filled with various delicious nuts.

This is a bait for clients as well. It speaks about your creativity. The more creative you are with the name, the better.

Chapter 3: Business Requirements

After you have perfected the flavor palette, you will have to attend to the business side of thing. This is where the legal and technical factors come in. This can be a bit tricky. Handle it with care, though because loopholes in this area may get you into trouble with the law.

Come up with your logo

First things first. You have to come up with a unique logo for your business. In this regard, a good graphic artist/designer will tell you that the logo must be simple yet beautiful enough that even if you print it as black and white in letters, it will still be striking.

At the same time, it should be reflective of the "character" of your cakes and business. It must talk about your niche. This way, your potential customers will easily know that it is them to whom you are actually making a pitch.

If you are not really good at this aspect, do not fret because you can always hire an expert to do the job for you. Seek the services of a graphic designer. S/he will help you convert your thoughts into an actual image or logo. If you already have a design in mind, then just tell him/her so s/he can provide the necessary input. On the other hand, if you have zilch, then just share your ideas with him/her so you can work it out until you finally achieve the logo that best fits your cake business.

In relation to this, you must also come up with a business card, template, and brochure. These should be patterned after your business logo and overall look. They will be used for the marketing and promotion of your business and baked goods. So do not forget the business name, contact information, goods offered, instructions for orders, and specific notes like the expiry date, etc.

Legal requirements

Next up, the legal requirements. In establishing a business, you will have to get a various permits starting from your area then moving upward to the State or national scope. Apart from that, you will also have to secure certification and necessary documents from concerned agencies.

Again, you have to remember here that different localities and states may have varying requirements. So you have to check first with the local authorities the rundown of the permits and legal papers you have to work on. Also, you have to be prepared for inspections.

Generally, you will have to register first with the agency tasked to oversee food hygiene and sanitation. Apart from that, it is a must to get in touch with the chamber of commerce for the business registration as a legal entity. Apply for the necessary licenses as dictated by them.

Dues

Lastly, you have to be mindful of your regular dues. You can hire a bookkeeper or accountant to take care of this if your business is already big. If not, have the in-house staff or secretary to attend to it. But if you are on your own, make sure that you are aware of your deadlines.

Among the things included here are taxes, rent, utility bills, and other government dues, among others.

Chapter 4: Marketing and Promotion

Another aspect to focus on is marketing and promotion. This is a tricky aspect. It does not end with being able to put up your cake business. In order for the latter to survive, especially with the tough competition in the industry, you have to master the next step which is marketing and promotion.

Find your niche

The key here is simple—find your niche and study it. Although yes, it is easier said than done, this is essential for effective marketing and promotion. The client base for cakes is quite big; after all, cakes are a staple for special occasions. But aside from that, they are wonderful desserts that almost everyone loves. You will surely not run out of customers.

But since there are also a lot of cake businesses out there, you have to find a particular target market first. This will be your specialty. There are a lot to choose from—gourmet cakes, baby cakes, wedding cakes, cupcakes, homemade cakes, vegan and gluten-free cakes, cakes for those on a diet, etc.

Packaging

Once you have found your niche, you have to learn how to entice your market. What is your selling point? That means you have to package your product with their interest in mind. The taste and overall look of your cakes should be in accordance with this. The same is true with the packaging—boxes, ribbons, stickers, and tags will come into play here.

Will you be using store-bought materials or will you have them custom-made? The important thing here is that you put your distinguishing mark, so do not forget your logo and business name. The same is true for your contact details. Your packaging should be able to incorporate all these three essential aspects.

Even the shape, texture and color of the materials you will use have an impact on the packaging. Will you be using a closed box with a flip top or a removable cover? Will you be incorporating a plastic cover on top so customers can have a sneak peek of what is inside the box?

In terms of colors, there are shades which actually make people hungry according to studies—these include red and orange. You may want to incorporate them. Also, you have to think of your theme. Will you go for pastel colors for a homemade appeal, or will you be playing with different shades?

Networking

Take advantage of your existing networks—this includes your family and friends. Start with them. Occasionally bring goodies to celebrations with your relatives and peers. Then snowball from there. When you have finally decided to go into formal business, ask for their help for referrals and recommendations.

Begin with small orders and special occasions. Make sure that you do well in your first orders because this will lay the groundwork for your reputation. You do not want to blow your chances for succeeding orders because you were unprofessional in your first try. So make sure that you only accept what you can do and make good on your commitments.

Also, you must bear in mind that free taste and samples is part of starting a business. So you will have to set aside a budget for that.

Eventually, it will pay off and you will be able to get your capital back. Just make sure though that you have the right audience during your introductory phase. These are the people who will not only buy your cakes, but also recommend them to other cake lovers or people who will need them for special as well as regular occasions.

When experimenting with your flavors, it also pays to have these free taste sessions—it is a cheaper form of market research. Get the feedback of those who got a free taste and collate them. Work from there in planning for improvements.

Social media

Last but not least, do not forget the power of social media. There is the ever reliable electronic mail or e-mail. But apart from that, venture into the famous and trendy social media platforms today—Facebook, Twitter, and Instagram. Here, you have to post the best photos and videos of your products. Also, make sure that you give regular updates so your followers will have something to look forward to.

In this regard, it is paramount that you pay particular attention to the quality of your photos and videos. Hire a professional if you can. You have to bear in mind that you eat with your eyes, too. In fact, you eat with your eyes first, so when you post photos, make them of great quality. They should be enticing enough to make the viewers drool and crave for your cakes.

Bazaars

Take part in bazaars. They can be a good way to start expanding your client base. Your existing network also has its limit, so you have to expand and explore outside options. Bazaars are a trusted means for this. Participate every once in a while. Just choose which will serve your purpose best. Joining bazaars can be a bit costly, though. There are times when you will be able to earn the amount that you spent, but sometimes, you will just break even. In any case, remember, it is all about your strategy.

Also, you have to bear in mind that some of your competitors will be there. Thus, you have to be prepared with your own gimmick. Be friendly. Do not just sit there; try talking to people as they pass by. Go out there and sell your goods and business.

And lastly, bring all the essentials. Do not forget your business cards and brochures as well. In fact, bring a lot of them and hand them out to as many people as possible. Some may not buy your cakes in the meantime, but that does not mean they will not give it a thought in the future. This is where the value of business cards and brochures come in.

Chapter 5: Logistics

Last but not least, you have to prepare the logistics. This includes not only the facilities, tools, and equipment, but the ingredients and other supplies as well.

Tools and ingredients

Baking involves a specific set of tools. Cake making and decorating is even more specific. Thus, you have to invest in the proper equipment. This will not only make production easier, it will make the entire process much more efficient. Through the help of the proper machines, you can work faster. This is very important especially with the bulk of cakes to be made for the daily operation of your cake shop, or during special occasions when orders are in bulk.

Decorating cakes are also done better if you have the proper tools. You do not have to buy the most expensive ones though; sometimes, the cheaper products are also good. You just have to choose them wisely. However, do not ever buy the ridiculously cheap ones because they tend to break easily.

Keep in mind that the tools you have are for the long term, so invest in things that will last. A lot of people take time and effort to save up in order to buy more sophisticated and durable equipment from the top brands. These are usually better than the cheaper versions which wear and tear quickly.

As for the ingredients, you have to consider that they are perishable. Do not buy more than what you can use because it is cheap. You have to balance it out with your needs though, so you always have to have items in stock. This way, you will not run out of the necessities, especially when you have rush orders. You cannot afford to keep rushing to a baking supplies store every time you have orders just because you did not have enough in your stock, unless of course the store is just across your house. But then again, what if they also run out of the things you need? Hence, you have to be prepared.

At the same time, be mindful of the expiration date. Sometimes, the amount that you saved when you bought ingredients in bulk is wasted because you have to throw some of the ingredients away since you were not able to use them before their expiration date.

Usually, it is better to buy in bulk, especially if you are doing a large scale production. It will even give you huge savings if you buy things in wholesale. But of course, you have to make sure that you have the orders for them. Here, it is important to set targets for your daily operation. How many cakes will you be making? How many of them will be on display? Then how many are made upon placement of order?

Make an everyday assessment. Plan out your operation the next day, the next weeks, and months even. This way, you can monitor your expenses, what you need, your targets, and how to achieve them. This is especially important once your business starts to expand. You do not want to ruin your reputation just because you were not able to meet client deadlines.

Storage and maintenance

Lastly, proper storage and maintenance of your tools is also important. It is not enough that you wash them after use; you also have to know how to stow them away properly. Speaking of washing your tools, you must be aware as well of the proper way to do that. There are tools and equipment that have parts which are not dishwasher-friendly. There are also those which cannot withstand heat, else they melt.

When it comes to storage, you have to make sure that you not only have ample space, but also the appropriate storage equipment. Keep in mind that you are dealing with food; hence, you have to make sure that your ingredients and tools are tucked in the proper storage areas so that they will not be contaminated. Tools must also be protected from rust. There are ingredients that have to be refrigerated. On the other hand, there are those which can be stored at room temperature.

Be mindful of these so you will not waste what are supposed to be long term investments. Also, this will impact on the safety of your food since improper storage can lead to contamination or insect infestation which will surely harm your clients' health. This is a good way not only to lose customers, but also get a lawsuit.

Chapter 6: Continue to Grow

It does not stop with putting up and opening your cake business. You must always strive for growth. This is not just for the business per se, but also for you as the owner and/or baker. The fact is, there are a lot of opportunities for growth in this industry.

You must continuously challenge yourself and perfect your craft. If you are hiring a pastry chef, then it is important as well that you learn to bake and not leave everything to the pastry chef. Be proactive. Whip something up in the kitchen and experiment. You may just instruct your pastry chef to perfect your concoctions.

On the other hand if you are the one who does the baking, constantly refining your flavors is a must; hand in hand with this is perfecting your decorating skills. And of course, do not forget to pay attention to your marketing and promoting techniques as well. As mentioned earlier, you must give your clients variety, so continuous experimentation is a must. Have other people taste your new concoctions and get as much feedback as you can. The latter is important to guide you.

There are people who find spending some alone time in the kitchen as a great relaxation method. They are happy when they bake. This is a must if you are going to venture into the cake industry.

Attending seminars and classes to hone your skills is also a great option you must consider. You can take part in one day classes in schools to learn something new. The internet is teeming as well with online tutorials. Baking groups—real or virtual—will also be of great help. Ideas shared therein can serve as your inspiration to come up with new concepts for your business.

You can also take master classes in good baking schools. This way, you can take your craft to higher levels. Your designs can be more intricate, your flavors more powerful. If you do not want to spend so much on these, there are always grants and scholarships that you can avail of.

Expand your cake shop

Continue going further. Once your cake shop is stable, you may want to expand it to be a café. After all, cakes and coffee are a great combination. It will also widen your client base. Just make sure though that you are still able to put premium on your cakes; they should be the star. You can then come up with your own coffee, tea, hot chocolate or other beverage mixes that will go well with the taste of your cakes.

Later on, you may want to open a couple of branches. Start small, then expand bit by bit. Remember to take it one step at a time. Make sure that the branch you are opening is well established before you move on to the next. Make ample preparations before you open another shop.

Some cake business owners also venture into teaching. You may want to start conducting your very own classes at a room on top of your cake shop. A lot of bakers venture into this in the long run. They want to impart their knowledge to novice bakers, and make a living out of this as well. If you want to offer free classes or have discounted rates, that will be a good thing, too.

Be resourceful, creative, and proactive. The opportunities for growth and expansion are just out there.

Chapter 7: Explore the industry

Last but not least, make it a point to explore the industry. As mentioned in the preceding chapter, take advantage of the opportunities that will come your way. There are a lot of them. Some examples of which are conferences, expos, and competitions.

Conferences and expos

There are regular conferences and expos held for and by cake entrepreneurs. There are similar events held for other food and beverage categories as well. Taking part in them is a good move to know more about the industry, learn the latest techniques and technology, and expand your network.

Since key players in the industry will be present in these gatherings, it is also a good opportunity to meet potential business partners and contacts. Thus, make it a point to put yourself out there. Meet other people and take advantage of the opportunity to talk business. Have your business cards, brochures, and sample products ready.

Conferences and expos involve product demonstration as well. You may want to look into these. It may be high time to have your mixer or oven replaced with the more updated and state of the art equipment that will make the production process faster, easier, and more efficient. Keep yourself up to date with the latest technological innovations so that you can distinguish which of them will help in your business.

You may also want to take advantage of the fact that products on display at these gatherings are offered at discounted prices because they come from the manufacturers themselves. So when you attend these gatherings, make sure you have your budget ready. On the other hand though, make sure that you spend wisely. Take note, there will be a lot of temptations there—beautiful and shiny equipment, low-priced ingredients, etcetera—but just buy what you need, or at least stay within your budget. If you have the money to spend for luxury or leisure, go ahead, but just keep it under control because otherwise, you may end up with busted pockets.

Another reason to join conferences and expos is the fact that you will find your competitors there. Thus, it can be an occasion to learn from them. Take part in healthy competition. Just take a look at their designs, and have a taste of their products. Find out if there are some improvements you can make to your own products, depending on your observation from other cake business owners and bakers. This does not mean though that you should pirate ideas--just get inspiration and tweak them to make them your own.

These gatherings are also a great opportunity to learn from the best in the field. In a lot of expos, experts do their own presentations and demonstrations. Be observant of these and take note of the things that will be useful for you and your business. Chefs will be sharing some of their secret ingredients and techniques. Take note of them and try to apply them in your own kitchen to see if they can work for you as well.

Competitions

Aside from the conferences and expos, you should also look into competitions. This is especially true if you are the baker of your business. Joining competitions can be a good way to put your business out there. It is also one form of promoting your business. Even if you lose, you already put your cake business' name on the map. At the same time, these competitions also provide you an opportunity to learn.

Joining competitions can also be good for the credentials of your cake business. Imagine, you can put different certificates, medals, and trophies as decors in your cake shop. But they are not just there for adornment, they are also there to boast of your success. Also, they speak about your cake shop's reputation. If you win, that will speak greatly of the taste and quality that you offer through your products.

If at first you do not succeed, keep trying. There is no harm in joining competitions. Just make sure that you are better prepared the next time you join one and you have learned so much more so you can bring better products to the table. Look at each competition as an opportunity to learn something new and make improvements for your own business.

Conclusion

Thank you again for downloading this book!

I hope this book was able to help you to learn the basics of putting up your own cake business, then moving on from there until expansion and continuous growth not only for the business, but also for you as the baker and owner.

Owning and running a cake business can be a lot of fun, especially if baking is your hobby. But at the same time, there are a number of factors that you have to consider in order to pave the way for your success.

It is also important to note that it does not end with putting up your own store front. Owning a cake shop involves continuous growth not just for the business itself, but also for you as its owner and baker. There are a lot of opportunities to expand horizons—take advantage of them. Strive hard to be the best in the field.

And now that you are armed with the necessary concepts, the next step is to apply what you have learned and wade your feet into the actual cake industry. Do not be afraid. Take the first step and make sure that you do the necessary follow through. It may be a rollercoaster ride, but in the end you will see how sweet the journey can be—literally and figuratively.

I'm maintaining a blog where you will find lot of wonderful cake and chocolate recipes, Please visit http://www.cakeandchocolateworld.com

Finally, if you enjoyed this book, then I'd like to ask you for a favor, would you be kind enough to leave a review for this book on Amazon? It'd be greatly appreciated!

Thank you and good luck!

www.ingramcontent.com/pod-product-compliance
Lightning Source LLC
Chambersburg PA
CBHW020714180526
45163CB00008B/3086